TOM THOMSON IN PURGATORY

Tom Thomson in Purgatory

Published by MARGIE, Inc. / IntuiT House *Poetry Series*

Senior Editor: James Wilson   Series Editor: Robert Nazarene

COVER ART: "Mazy Avenues" by James Kuiper

Manufactured in The United States of America

ISBN 0-9719040-5-7   paperback

TOM THOMSON IN PURGATORY

Troy Jollimore

For my parents

Contents

FOREWORD
by BILLY COLLINS

TOM THOMSON IN PURGATORY falls
gracefully into the American tradition of the extended
persona poem, a pack of contenders led by John
Berryman's Henry of his DREAM SONGS. Troy
Jollimore knows how to trot forth a character as distinct as
one who might be encountered in sharply rendered
fiction, but here in only a sketch of lines, sometimes
within the discrete container of the sonnet. What engages
the reader most is a sensibility that can combine the
audacity of Tom Thomson himself with the restrained
etiquette of the formalism that guides these poems and
shapes them into statuesque entities. Also this poet knows
how to use form—often a pentameter beat—to give
dimension and scale to his elastic and expansive
imagination which is capable of startling leaps typically
from the mundane to the philosophical and back.

Of course, we know and delight in the knowledge
that Tom Thomson is a verbal phantom, the result of the
poet's word-spinning, but at the same time we lean
forward to believe in him—our hero for the moment, a
man of the hour.

What is most affective is that Troy Jollimore himself
believes in this Tom Thomson (whose common name
echoes John Jones) and relies on him as a model of
ventriloquism when the poet cannot speak for himself.
Reading this book, you are bound to take both Tom
Thomson and his creator to your heart and to savor the
miscellany of other poems that make up this superb
collection.

FROM THE BOY SCOUT MANUAL

If you penetrate to some warm recess under a cliff in the woods, you will be astonished at the amount of summer life that still flourishes there. No doubt more of the summer's life than we are aware thus slips by and outmaneuvers the winter, gliding from fence to fence.

Henry David Thoreau, *Journals*, Nov. 19, 1850

MOCKINGBIRD AND
WHIPPOORWILL

In July it occurs to the mockingbird
that many a human would love to lay
a rough, unfeathered hand upon
its faculty of flight;
and so it takes to the ground, grows round
and mothlike, and becomes,
so far as any human eye can tell,
a whippoorwill.

In August it befalls the whippoorwill
to wonder whether, given its love
for the tip-topped tree, its peculiar penchant
for singsong, those disturbing dreams
in which it swoops and careens as if
aflame, its actual name
might not be of an altogether different feather:
in a word, *mockingbird.*

AFTER

If we must speak of each other, let it be
in the forms that monarchs and generals use
to refer to their rivals; as if each were known
to the other only through field reports
and classified intelligences. Let it be
in tones of wariness, grudging respect, and,
where permitted, mutual admiration.
Let our campaign be conducted on these terms.

And if people speak of the 'break-up,'
let us hear in that the cold overtones
of the word as applied to a glacier: how,
when the ice began to shudder and crack,
new light found an entry, and the gleaming designs,
evolving each moment, each moment formed
a kaleidoscope view—a lens through which
an eerie and unforeseen world finally offered
itself to be seen—as the fragments, mindless
and pure, frigid yet free, plunged
to the sea, that vast, that resolute,
that insensate, that insatiable sea.

TROUT QUINTET

1

Where water meets water,
where rain hangs lead-heavy for days
before finally deciding to harden and fall,
where the nearest road is sixty miles away
and that a narrow track of gravel,
where the lake is as still as a photograph
and has never been photographed,
where the trout return in accordance with a schedule
that is not a human schedule,
following a water-bearing brain-map,
a hard-wired river route, an instinct chart,

Tom Thomson is playing solitaire.
Each time he loses,
he throws his cards into the water.
Each time he wins
he catches a trout.

2

He likes this place
because the satellites cannot see it
and the water is pure.
He likes this place
because it is where the trout come,
where they stop.
He likes this place
because parsley and wild tomatoes
grow naturally on the banks.
He likes the way
his canoe fits the water.
He likes the way
the water fits the earth.

Is Tom Thomson a figure of legend?
Tom Thomson is a living totem pole.
Is Tom Thomson larger than life?
Four men could stand in Tom Thomson's shadow,
smoking cigars and talking about baseball.

One night four men came for him
carrying guidebooks and sawed-off shotguns.
A week later their Chevy Suburban was found.
The motor was running. The left turn indicator blinking.
The glove box was filled with trout.

3

"There is much joy to be found
in the imprecise usage of words."
Tom Thomson disagrees. He slams his bottle
down on the wooden table. The wood,
anticipating the bottle's arrival,
splinters in advance.

Who would call a trout a salmon?
But words are arbitrary.
Who would call a trout an iceberg?
Call it what you want, it will not come.

Tom Thomson's grunt clears the forest of birds.
His laughter frightens the gods.
The philosopher Thales devised a method
of measuring Tom Thomson by taking the length
of his shadow at the moment when a normal man's shadow
was as long as the man was tall.

Tom Thomson snorts at philosophers.
He has never touched a tape measure.
He eyeballs every measurement,
and is astoundingly accurate.
He measures once, cuts once.
He speaks seven languages. He has perfect pitch.

4

A hesitant breeze brings mist from the north.
The location of the sun during the past
three days is a matter of some controversy.
The lake is stiffening with trout. They are pouring
in from all over. The sound of a paddle
entering and pushing the water aside
slowly corrupts the silence.

Tom Thomson stops, lets go the paddle,
reaches over the side and makes
a secret mark on a rock.
The mark indicates that this is a place
Tom Thomson has been, and will come to again.

Have you ever seen a man murdered?
Once. I saw it in a mirror.
And did he remind you of your father?
I can't answer that question. Nor any other.

5

Tom Thomson likes to pull a trout from the water
and fry it up with parsley and wild tomatoes.
The recipe is from his favorite restaurant
on Yonge Street in Toronto. Tom Thomson
eats there once a year. He does not need
a reservation. He has left a secret
mark upon the door.

What is Tom Thomson's secret mark?
What does it look like?

I can't tell you.

Come on.

Let me tell you something: the trout
that come to the place where water meets water
are the same trout every year.
They are not born. They do not die.

Impossible.

All I can do is tell you.

What of the sign. Can you give me a hint?

I already have.

Tell me something.
Is that Tom Thomson playing the piano?

That is not Tom Thomson playing the piano.
Tom Thomson plays no instrument. He does not
sing. He knows no poetry.
He can't even read. Tom Thomson
spends each night alone, listening to the phonograph,
looking at old family photos. Or so they say.

GLASS

When was it that he first saw something shatter,
and learned, in that instant, so much about the world?
He must have seen the little webs of glittering glass
a hundred times before that, on the sidewalks and streets,
on the playground concrete, and supposed them to have been
deposited like dew. Or they might have coalesced
from the empty, rigid air. But then, something broke
before his eyes, and from that moment everything was clear.
What a shock it must have been! What a surprise
to see that things end, that things are transformed
into other things . . . It must have been so much
for a child to grasp. And what of water,
which looks like glass but does not shatter?
And what of air? And what of the soul?
Are we glass or are we water? And where
does the child go who wants this answered?

He went to a field of yellow grass and thistle
behind the old train station and sat alone
for hours. The place was alive with the ominous,
omnivorous hum of the neighborhood insects,
and the waving, muttering grass seemed to capture
the heat of the sun the way a puddle
of water will capture and hold one small corner
of sky's panorama. In the distance, noises:
barking dogs, traffic, groaning lawn mowers.
He learned the beginnings and the ends of noises,
and how the silence that goes before
differs from the silence that comes after.

And he took this knowledge back to his home
where there was a different kind of silence:
the long pauses between his mother's questions
and their responses; the careful, weary
evening reticence of his father;
the quiet neglect of books and small objects,

18

untouched, left alone to be what they were.
In his corner room he made notes, kept journals,
and charted a course of investigation
as, outside, the world passed by, a featureless
ocean, identical in all directions.

FIREFLIES

As if they could be summoned by a word –
one you might have spoken, or perhaps, misspoken
(it's been known to happen) – in the mist-charged air,
the blue lead-tinted tinge of not-quite-remembering
that is early evening – they appear.

Live embers, greenish gold. Tiny sky-writers.
Light forgers, within whose delicate chambers
the elements of a cold flame are brought together.
The wind breathes them. The rigid stars above
envy the way their nervous constellations

make and then remake themselves. It is perhaps
some certain grade of silence they await,
or some precise earth-tilt, some just-so slant
of the sun's declining final rays, that sets
the temperature that sends the call that brings them out.

And suddenly they are everywhere – the air,
the bushes, the sluggish river water, the eyes
of people you pass, nodding, then stop to wonder
whether they meant, as you did, by your nod,
to acknowledge the little lamps, or something else altogether.

The bugs themselves seem to acknowledge nothing,
but go on blinking in their binary code:
on-off, one-zero. Poised, aflutter, between two
thoughts, two possibilities, each one
desiring our belief, though they cannot both be true.

TOBEKOBEKON

The feelings you thought were genuine
were purchased at a discount
from a supplier
in a city with a name something like
Tobekobekon, Ohio.
A city where there are more cafés
than people, and residents gather
under the eaves of the bridge which connects them
with their sister city
in New Jersey.
In these small groups they confess their sins,
passing cigarettes in circles.
My supplier was a kind man
who kept a large family
and whose irrational attraction
to large sea mammals
would lead to his untimely demise.
I am telling you this
so you will know what it is
that wakes me at four every morning,
wanting you
more than drugs, or sleep, or peace.

HOW TO GET THERE

You could veer off now, but it might be best
to keep to the route you've been following
for just a bit longer. That will give you a chance
to finish your book-on-tape, drain your coffee,
and ask yourself for the thousandth time
"Why didn't I just stay home?" Up ahead
you will come to a highway, eight or ten lanes of traffic,
a rainbow of car-colors, huge alien
billboards, drive-through espresso stands
like so many *Monopoly* hotels.
Make a break for the other side.
Swing as far left as you can go — *farther!* —
and drive down that narrow country lane
for twenty or thirty miles. When you get
to the river, the bridge will be out. A dog
will appear as if summoned. This is your sign
to turn back, to look for the tiny side road
that you should have turned onto before, but could not,
because it's only visible once you've passed it.
When you reach the village
(the cluster of white houses)
stop and discard the map.
Also get rid of the passengers.
From here on in they'd only weigh you down.
Leave them by the side of the road. You'll need
a new identity. Call yourself 'Gary.'
Say that you're in 'insurance.'
You'll be due for a maintenance check about now;
use the time to visit the nearby diner
that sells the best cheesecake and worst coffee in the whole
Tri-State area. Flirt with the waitresses.
It might get you slapped but they'll love you for it.
By now you'll have lost too much time: you'll have to
revise destinations. Though in fact
it won't make any difference. Remember,
anyone with a knowledge of physics will tell you

that the road not taken would have led you to the same place; or else, it was never accessible at all.

THE HEIGHT OF MY POWERS

This particular shade of blue
is what brings it out in me —
the morning sun, the books you brought
to breakfast. The simple dress

that you say looks like an apron, that I won't
admit how much I adore, because
I don't want you to stop wearing it.

Did you dream last night? I ask.
No one smiles like the Mona Lisa,
you say, not anymore.
Perhaps. But perhaps it's just this:
no one can tell a joke like da Vinci.

No matter. The day has officially begun.
I am at the height of my powers.
And if I can't make *you* smile like that
I'll eat these slippers. Those books. Whatever you like.

ROSES INVERTED

The roses that grow in that stony ground
send their roots straight up, and their blossoms down.

Their sun-seeking roots anchor them in the air,
but they find neither water nor nourishment there.

Their leaves stretch toward the planet's hot core.
But the earth's inner engine radiates more

heat than it does light, so that, to their surprise,
they find that they cannot photosynthesize.

They are white as milk. Up among the stones,
the pale roots linger like the half-buried bones

of abandoned camels licked clean by the sands.
Yet the underground flowers that open like hands

are brazen and bright. They unfurl like flags.
Among the miniature caverns and crags

just beneath the surface, these banners gather,
sheltered from sun, from stars, from weather—

sheltered, too, from admirers; hidden from any
appreciative eye. And there are so many!

They are thoughts we attempted to utter, but failed.
Or confessions of love: folded, stamped, never mailed.

THE TURTLE

ventures an eye
into the realm of air.
Nobody's there—

only the sky,
upside down lake where
strange fish float by.

★ ★ ★

Silent, still,
wedged like a shim
between the two realms

his reptilian will
is urgent and grim.
The gap is filled.

★ ★ ★

Picture them, stacked under the ground:
he and his kind, all the way down.

ROSENCRANTZ AND GUILDENSTERN ARE DEAD, RUINED BY READING THE CANTOS OF EZRA POUND

Or, Song of My Shelf

1

Under the volcano
in the garden of the North American martyrs
two serious ladies
left out in the rain
repair
the crooked timber of humanity.

2

God knows
the heart never fits its wanting.
God knows
love is the crooked thing.
God knows
the information:
all things, all at once.
God knows
the untouchable
dreams of distant lives.

3

When one has lived a long time alone
on the great Atlantic rainway,
and the stars were shining,
the importance of what we care about
lies
with ignorance,
divine comedies,
difficult loves.

4

Why, Brownlee left
The Book of Laughter and Forgetting
at Swim-two-birds.
Ulysses annotated
The Annotated Lolita
at weddings and wakes.
Praise
the cunning man,
the engineer of human souls.
Praise
the dispossessed,
the man who mistook his wife for a hat.

5

While England sleeps,
Kant and the platypus
kiss in the Hotel Joseph Conrad.
The boy on the step
second guesses
the fortunate traveller.
After Ovid,
who will run the frog hospital?

6

The world as I found it—
the world at large—
points, in time,
to the wedding:
a vision
of love and shadows,
first love and other sorrows.

7

What is justice?
A guide for the perplexed.
A thought in three parts.
A dream of mind.
The heart is a lonely hunter
on a cold road:
blizzard of one.
Must we mean what we say?
The horse's mouth
lies.
Consider the oyster.

8

If on a winter's night a traveler,
coming into the country
on a pale horse,
opening the hand
the rest of the way
for the union dead,
travels
with ignorance
of love and other demons,
love and its place in nature,
seeing things –
home truths,
signals of distress –
as if
the half-life of happiness
is 5,
as if
the world is the home of love and death –
if on a winter's night a traveler
travels,
can you stand to be blessed?
Can you hear, bird,
what we owe to each other?

9

Little friend, little friend,
fall on your knees.
Let it come down.
Call it sleep.

THE DIVERS

There is the silent sea
like a huge unblinking azure eye

seeing itself from within.
And there are the dark shapes that move

through the scene as if pulled by strings.
Slow, everything happens slowly here

as if hardly happening at all.
If one died here, would it be real?

Or would one wake as if from a dream
in a well-lit room up above?

No, a death here would surely be real.
The ocean is like a death,

a vast ending to all things.
And some of us have heard bells down here,

far away, and all around.

The sea floor is not like land,
or a thing that ever was land.

It is like a huge body, lying down.

Not dead, but in a deep sleep.
We make our way over its skin

moving as precisely as thieves
trying not to trip an alarm.

Each diver is a planet:
he carries his atmosphere on his back.

And the water is the brother of outer space.
A darkness. A hole in the lung.

DEVOUR

The wretched brackens and eelgrass
that choke the knee-deep water are jealous
of their brother, the bladderwort.

The bladderwort, through years of aching
desire and discipline – the painful
stumble-in-the-dark of evolution –

has taught itself a new and wicked
trick: to eat. To take the world
inside itself and hold it there

until world disappears and the plant
surges with strength, only to sicken
with want again and devour again

and again. Devour, my sweet, devour.
Let the world enter and become you.
Taste it, the animate earth, the harsh tang.

COSMOLOGY

Weather maps, orbital glare of suns –
I have my place
in this grand, invisibly
orchestrated toy,

and if, for a moment,
I step away
and watch myself from
the outside

it is only through a window
in my head
that is, these days,
more often closed than open.

Power and light.
A meeting of eyes.
Love, the black box
in the works

pulled out of the wreckage
and puzzled over.
I dance. I recite.
I am ruled by dark matter.

LIGHT

1

When the gates were finally thrown open and the world was
  filled with light
no one, at first, could see a thing – it was overwhelming:
from utter, infinite darkness into blazing, limitless light –
but then they began to adjust, and to look on things for the first
  time.
And they were amazed to discover that some things – ice, to
  take an example –
looked the way they felt; and that some – like rain, for
  instance –
looked they way they sounded; and that the wind, which could
  feel like rushing water
and sound like a wounded animal, did not, at least for the most
  part,
look like anything at all. It was all so new to them
that they declared a public holiday and closed down all the
  shops,
the banks, the government offices, the libraries, the schools,
and they just walked around and looked at things, then gathered
  to compare notes,
and each person wondered whether or not he ought to admit to
  the others
that he wasn't sure that he liked it, that he felt just a bit afraid.

2

All that time they'd been carrying eyes around, not knowing
  what they were for.
It was good to know. It was good, they all agreed, to have that
  settled.

3

If you start with a burning candle in a dark room and add a
     mirror
you would then have two candles, which, he reasoned, would
     make it twice as bright;
so, adding an infinite number of mirrors, you'd have unlimited
     energy
which, he mused to himself, it would be possible to harness
and hook up to a city, or a machine – maybe a weapon,
and what if it fell into the wrong hands? —but he'd be
     careful...
He made extensive notes; he drew up a detailed proposal
which he practiced presenting to his brothers, to the cat,
to the gardenia on the patio. That was the day she left him.

4

The light that shoots from the sun across the earth's surface like
     a beam from the eye
of a lighthouse, and licks and adorns the tops of the tallest
     buildings, blaring through windows
like the shockwave of a thunderclap and falling on those still
     sleeping
and on those in love and on those who have risen early so that
     they might make love
in these few moments before the first cog of the great day
     catches
is the same light which, just a few moments later, tilts and
     begins to fall
into the cracks of the ancient city and onto the streets below,
falling on parents and children, falling on plazas, falling on
     bicycles,
falling on newspapers, sidewalks and street signs, falling on
     fences and puddles,
falling on clocks and bypasses, falling on restaurants and
     churches,

falling on the forgotten, falling on the neglected, falling on
    an old man
who, distracted, raises his hand to his brow and looks to the sky
and sees a vast and dispersing crowd of sun-kindled ravens or
    crows
bursting into the air, each one glowing as if it were tarred with
    fresh pitch,
livid and ink-black, a flurry of exclamation marks!

FROM THE BOY SCOUT MANUAL

for Donal Power

When lost in forests, keep in mind
that moss is always most full and bright
on the side of the tree that faces the nearest
major urban area.
And mushrooms tilt to magnetic north
during spring tides, and away in the neap.

Deer can be attracted
by the sound of a low and gentle voice
speaking anything at all, especially
rhyming verse. (Browning is best.)
If you are truly hungry, they
will allow themselves to be captured and eaten.

Water can be boiled in
a pot, or if you have no pot,
over a fire in your cupped hands.
The backs of the hands should be kept moist
during this procedure, and it is best
to keep your eyes closed and think of the ocean.

There are many berries that can be eaten,
and on which humans may subsist
for weeks, if need be. To determine
which ones hold poison, place a berry
beneath your head when you go to sleep.
If you dream of it, it is safe to eat.

Water may be located under the earth
by swinging a weight on the end of a string,
releasing it, and digging where
it falls. If gold, jewels, or currency
are turned up during the process, they
belong to the Scout who owns the shovel.

SPRING FORWARD, FALL BACK

In November the hours are slower:
winding-down weather, the fresh lather
of a first snow. The winter,
with its months of hospital afternoons

waits huddled just over the border.
And ice will make all the distances
that much further. Speak now, kiss now
before the river freezes altogether.

A PLEA FOR SILENCE

Did I neglect to mention
the first snow in the mountains?

Each faltering flake a parachute
on a doomed mission.

Did I forget to tell
of the spring melt?

The slow, stammering madrigal
of the waning icicle,

the soft *sluice* of rain water
through the rain gutter –

did I fail to report these things?
And does it matter?

The door that opens, opens.
We do not make it happen

by seeing it, or saying it.
Better that we keep quiet,

and listen for the music
in the creek's swift static.

The river, the snow-laden tree,
the massing of clouds over hills –

these things are fragile. We
only corrupt them when we tell

their stories. Leave them be.
Let them speak for themselves.

TOM THOMSON IN PURGATORY

The gods cannot afford to leave a man in the world who is privy to any of their secrets. They cannot have a spy here. They will at once send him packing. How can you walk on ground when you can see through it?

Henry David Thoreau, *Journals*, March 12, 1852

Prologue: Tom Thomson in Perspective

Let's see . . . He was in love. *How much?* Oh, much,
and fairly often. *More than once?* For sure.
With what? A woman, often. *The same one?*
Sometimes, and sometimes not. *And with what else?*
With life. *His own?* Yes, being the one he knew
up close, but not his only; something in him
lifted above that close-hemmed-in horizon
to try and take in Life Itself, and love,
to the extent he could, that too. *And did*
that work? Well, no – his powers were too puny.
But still, he tried. That has to count for something.

Yes, that seems only fair. Let's put him down, then,
as Honorable Failure and an Honest Attempt.
Yes, I can live with that. And him? *He'll have to.*

I

Tom Thomson in Love

Love pushed him sidewise through the bleary nights.
It flew at him like storms. He tried to learn
to overcome, to do without, but could,
he found, not; nor cigarettes, neither. He stuck
to them like glue. Opinions stuck to him
and drugged him down into the muck. Always asked he
what lay so deep down there — well now he knows:
it's *him* — it's he himself, goes down so far
and lies at bottom and takes not one breath
all winter, like a turtle. Him, who looks
upward through bottoms of glass-bottomed boats
and so on into sky, sky up as he is down,
sky blue as he, and free as he is not.
People say "My friend" to him, but just ironically.

Tom Thomson in Turmoil

Lay down them projects for the crackling stars.
The hourglass sifts itself. Stars sprawl and blaze
in every each direction, and their howl
torments him into sleep. There was a point
from which they all emerged, of infinite mass,
through which he right now passes possibly through,
knowing it not. But then, what does he know?
And what could tell he to another ear?
Ears tilt away from him now when he speaks,
and people form strange patterns, fields, as if
a magnet he, and iron filings they.
"Lay down," he just repeats, "them projects." He
gives often to himself advice, and trusts
himself, though less these days, to get it right.

Tom Thomson in Hiding

Trusts himself less, but more than others do:
when he an elevator boards, they stand
off to one side and keep an eye on him,
suspicious-like; when he picks up a phone
a little click lets him know someone else
is listening, too. Meanwhile, spy satellites
fly so low overhead they almost graze
and take away a layer of his skin.
He therefore cringes, hunches, don't look up,
contemplates fake moustaches and dark shades,
scurries from house to car, inside whose tin
and plastic shell he feels less vulnerable.
There is a war afoot: Intelligence
versus intelligentsia. *This* he knows.

Tom Thomson in Between Women

There was a woman, some few months ago.
She left some things around. He finds them, still:
books stuffed flush into shelves; a pair of shoes;
a folder full of notes. Perhaps she needs,
he thinks, these crucial-looking notes. I ought
to call, perhaps. But does not call. For she
ought to have called, and called him she has not.
He shouts it: "Called me She has not!" He likes
these words, their vim, their final-sounding tone;
though what he likes these days, he's noticed, tends
to bother and provoke — that's why he likes it so:
He seeks bad tastes, foul scents, ugly tableaux,
lays head in gutters, travels high and low,
and learns by going where he hates to go.

Tom Thomson in His Office, Thursday Afternoon

Fills out grant applications. Honestly.
Although they asked him not to. That's, you know,
against the rules. Is honesty, that is.
And knows he therefore will not one red cent
get from them this year. Nor desires to.
Rejection is his muse. He thrives on it!
Who else can say they thrive on anything?
These days, that is. (His father's phrase.) But he's
more strong than they by far: For he can smile
and hoist a planet onto shoulder, he
can laugh at pain (and knows more pain than they) –
more pain, more love, more lust, more everything!
He is made stronger by what does not kill him.
And what does kill him, makes him stronger still.

Tom Thomson in Search of Lost Time

"These days." His father's phrase. That's as opposed
to "them" days, "those" days, ah, the good old days
he's heard about . . . He was not quite alive
back then. There was this kid that had his name.
Them days was quite exceptional: JFK
was king, dethroned by Sir Muhammed Ali,
and service stations lived up to the name.
Fish tasted better, and was cheaper too,
and nothing, not even dinosaurs, was extinct.
There was no sex, of course, but had there been,
it would have been *fantastic* –
                     – but he fears
it was his coming out into the world
that jarred it out of place, that put an end
to those days. Then: these days came roaring in . . .

Tom Thomson in Limbo (1)

Big fish eat little fish. Everywhere so.
And little fish find small new happy life
inside big fish. Big fish, meanwhile, is king
of little pond. And so the cycle go.

Go on and on, as cycles do. Big pond
goes also by the name of 'ocean,' see.
And as for oceans, there is only one,
but go by different name in different eye.

It's time, he says, at long last speaking true,
It's time that cuts me down and lays me low.
And gazes out, half-hoping to descry

some bobbing head stuffed stiff with little facts
to guide him home. And ocean, meanwhile, do
its work. Yes, patient ocean slay him slow.

53

Tom Thomson in Situ

Half of his neighbors are half-there at best,
in this dull plastic streetscape improvised
from the last remnants of some *actual* life.
Still, though it cost him dearly to admit,

he likes it here: from balcony he can see
his favorite deli, second favorite bar,
and in the distance, on a bright, clear day:
the Gates of Hell. Hell, if he squint through 'scope,

those infamous inscriptions coalesce:
Abandon all hope ye who enter here
and *Absolutely no outside food or drink* . . .

And what of Heaven? Must it, too, not be?
Same distance, opposite direction? But
his view don't face that way. *That's* speculation.

Tom Thomson in Denial

OK, so even if the mean IQ
stay where it stay, or even take a plunge
(as what passeth for entertainment, art,
opinion, and/or driving indicate),
still, one might think, the sheer supply of souls
ought to imply a corresponding glut
of geniuses. There ought, by Tom's rough count,
to be at least three Einsteins, and a good
one-and-a-quarter Shakespeares. But then where's
they hiding? Sitting on their secret mas-
terpieces, biding precious time? Or simply
lost in vast hubbub, parade of noise
in which Tom's own brain bobbles like a cork?
(Should'e file, perhaps, a Missing Persons report?)

Tom Thomson Indisposed

He's been in bed a week. A week's a long
time for someone in the prime of life
to spend in bed. But oh, those aches and pains!
A flare-up of Abacist's Elbow's cramped
his tennis game. His prosopagnosia, too,
is worse than ever: just barely can he place
that haunted-eye banshee that throws back, twice as hard,
his bathroom mirror stare. *I often grieve*
that I should grieve so much. He's been like this
since his provider cut from stream to drip
his life-support supply of bite-sized tabs
of Ecstasy, Relief, and Consolation
whose tiny kisses were the helium
that buoyed, once, his void, balloonish dome.

Tom Thomson in Limbo (2)

Loves himself in the morning. Hates himself
before the day is done. How to this cycle break?
How readjust this hijinxed world? How ease
large want into small income? How forgive?
How catch attention of a pretty eye?
How sign his name? How speak the truth? How live?

Time goes on. And ashamed he is to say
how time goes on. As if it might be paused
if only he the password had. He's plagued
by whispers – some soft, nagging voice he knows,
some language he does not. Comes as he turns
away by half – the room was empty, so
he thought; there ain't nobody here but me.
And even me, I'm none too sure about.

Tom Thomson Intoxicated

It sickens me to think
of all that I would have to drink
to clear a path from my one-room
apartment to her island home

and those vast wastes of tide that lie
between our two worlds – how can I
with oceans hope to do battle,
when all my ships are in bottles?

Raising them to my loose lips
I set sail on what liquid slips
from their necks down my throat.
After three, I am usually afloat.

It happens so often, the local mob
has taken to calling me 'Bob' . . .

Tom Thomson in Bed

Each night ride he his damp nostalgia-bed
into dark territories vast with vast
and hideous with memory-sculpted pain.
At openings where man without a past
might slip through like a fish, he jams and sticks,
twisted in harsh contortions – calls for help,
but only man in hearing range (himself)
does not awake or stir. Slimed slick with kelp,
he sees the crew of wretched craft, his life,
swimming like dogs toward the farther shore,
and strikes out for the opposite compass point.
(Surely they can't *all* drown . . .) But ocean floor
call to him like lost love, and down he goes.
Always asked he what lay there – now he knows.

II

Tom Thomson in the Morning

Wake with a start. Cold sweat-doused sheets. Good morning.
Close eyes, go over molecules one by one:
all present and accounted for. The dragon
of one more day stretched out before him, set
to be faced down and, in the end, laid low
with his good blade (which he's with guile disguised
as leather briefcase.) Into hot shower now,
slough off and steam-dissolve debris of night
that coats pale skin, yet try not to let pop
bubble of optimistic morning hope.
(Realistically – but he must hide from this –
the calculus do not support his knighthood:
he has inflicted more distress on damsels
than saved them from. The dragon, friends, *c'est Tom*.)

Tom Thomson in a Religious Quandary

Standing by fencepost tries to force a love
equal and for all persons.
                                    It don't come.
He love some people more than others. Hang
your head for that, bad Tom. A saint you ain't.
Has he been baptized? This he can't recall;
all documents rest resolutely vague
upon this point — though some rough incident
involving water and a man with robes
do hover in his memory like a cough.
A Buddhist, then? But they's cucumber-cool
in face of circumstance, whereas his style
alternates fits of gusto and despair.
He is the Church of Tom: sneakers his pulpit,
each sneeze a sermon, his remorse his prayer.

Tom Thomson in His Library

Bookplates, he useth not. Nor needs he to.
Reason the First: all his books share his scent,
a musk of salt-sea air, pine-redolent,
and hint of freshly doused campfire (suggest-
ing liberty to some, but to the rest
the reek of disappointment.) Crack the spine
and sniff: you'll know if from his cache it came.
Reason the Next: he has not loaned a book
to anyone for ten plus years. For no
one reads no more, and fewer people still
read what he reads, or feel the slightest pull
to transact business – giftings, borrowings –
with this musty old man whose books all smell
of salt, of lonesome woods, of drenched dead flames.

Tom Thomson In Limbo (3)

Each thing done is a thousand things not-done:
to read Frost is to not-read Henry James
or Keats and/or Rimbaud or Heisenberg . . .
(Calculus floors him. Physics spins his mind
beyond all equilibrium.) But worse,
to read anyone else's books is to
not-write his own. But why, when others' songs
fill all the airwaves full, should lack of song
on his own part make him feel shameful so?
If every ear already is stuffed dumb,
why want a voice? (He knows what *she'd* suggest:
pure egotism.) "In silence can man best
preserve his own integrity," fortune
from fortune cookie say. And he say: "   ."

Tom Thomson in Orbit

His enemies take comfort in his pain.
So tries to hide it from them. Hides himself,
for pain is of himself the visible part.
It is the craters and the so-called seas
(for they are dry as chalk and bone dust) whose
expanses occupy his surface. Poor Tom,
he is an open sore, orbiting round
an earth he thought was sun, until he found
she was in orbit round a man she could
not have, nor he bear. O it doth blow his mind,
this revolution of Copernican
dimensions. No wonder his path in life's
so hard to calculate. (He keeps his face
always to her.) No shock he can't think straight.

Tom Thomson in a Brand New Suit

Having no product – nothing to promote –
he's never taken serious the thought
that advertising could assist his cause.
What matters what they think of me? he muse,
when my warehouse is empty, and my staff
sent packing long ago? Filed Chapter Nine,
did he, emotional-wise, more than once,
and meant to get out of the sorry trade
all altogether. Now, though, fingers he
a snappy hat, and thinks to self, *perhaps,*
if thought they there was something underneath,
a man, a soul, not just a coat on stick,
perhaps . . . And ad man smile. "There ain't no hole
so deep it can't be covered up with style."

Tom Thomson in Vogue

With Pyramids behind, and with a glass
of some bright liquid sharp with fissioning sheen
in hand, he small talk make with shiny babe
as Photo Man for Hot New Magazine

the shutter clicks, and captures cover shot.
His stock is rising. What's he saying, though?
Ain't no one listening to a word – and him,
he listening least of all. But cares he? No.

He take his stunt double to lunch. He find
a gold doubloon behind his ex-wife's ear.
His writer friends seek agents. *He's* afraid
the agents will find him – they's drawing near,

swords drawn, to cut short his lush quarter-hour.
(Already tilts he like famed Pisa's tower.)

Tom Thomson, Intermittently

His car start when a coin toss come up heads.
His cell phone cut out when a dog pass by,
or cloud, or traveling salesman, or when he
pronounce a word that's from the French derived.
His fax machine work perfect – half the week
(Thursday through Sunday noon.) His shoes fit fine
so long as One Anointed Chair is oc-
cupied by Democrat. (But when Repub-
licans get in, TV reception clears.)
His vision's twenty-twenty, long as he
confine himself to gazing back. But when
he twist his neck to see the Coming Soons,
the great tailwind that from the future blows
douses squidged-open eyes with blears and tears.

Tom Thomson In Process

The scene: election booth. A private space,
where democratic citizen can dwell
alone with what thoughts he's allowed to have.
He's been here quite a while. Not that he don't
know who to choose, or what to do – he *knows*
decisively he must reject it all:
candidates, process, the entire shebang.
"Love it or leave it" – well, upstairs he va-
cated some time ago. Built a small hut
in his own mental woods, retired there. Now
gets news by post and radio. They sing
their tale: so much rewards for having rewards,
so few for being right. The *next* time round,
he'll check the box that says "I told you so."

Tom Thomson in Despair

That half the People say "the *parking* brake"
while th'others call it the *emergency* brake
suggests to him a Grand Divide so deep,
so chasmic, so potentially cataclysmic,
it might as well be continental. Could
good Jefferson, had he but half foreseen
the distance that would separate the tribes
have held out hope for a united state?
The lion wants to lie down, but not with lamb.
(With lamb *chops*, on the other hand . . .) No peace
obtains 'twixt dog and man, 'twixt red and blue . . .
The state of his *own* union's bad enough:
feels he, these days, like he's split into two.
(Or five, or twelve. On *good* days, only two.)

Tom Thomson in Doubt

The plan fell through. Nor would he (that is, He)
admit that there had even been a plan.
He didn't sign his work. Remained He mum.
Still did the people speculate. The prea-

chers say: "Have faith. He's up there." They contest:
"I talked to Him last night. He just was here.
He stepped out for a minute." People bought it
(some) or made as if they did (the rest).

But Tom could not. *If He is,* puzzled he,
He must not want us to believe. He knew,
like any good executive in chief,
that Plausible Deniability

matters above all else. *That settles it, then:*
nothing is settled. Or will be. Amen.

Tom Thomson Intransigent

Waste not? Want not? Dear Tom waste all he got
and wants he even more. A point of pride:
no man can match the vast of his desire.
What he *refuse* to do is waste away,
nor fade he, nor recede; his earthbound booth
will signal 'occupied' so long as he
a breath can suck down. So wait your damn turn,
all you dear unborn embryos, you soon-
to-be carbon-based life forms, you who hope
a space will soon appear; for stubborn Tom
refuse to shuffle off to Buffalo
or anywhere beyond this mortal coil.
He's not so much, in terms of looks or brawn,
but he's got sticking power, does dear Tom.

Tom Thomson in Excess

But is it fair? Why gets *he* to exist,
this eco-terrorist, devouring air
and food and alcohol and warmth and world
like it's a going-out-of-business sale?

Why he, who whine without relent at life,
should get so much of it? It seems *unjust.*
But wait. Hold on a second there. Yes, Tom,
he think that life's a bitch. But understand,

he *loves* that bitch. And she, he thinks, loves him,
at least on every second day, or fourth.
Or, at the very least, the way she grab
his neck and kiss his lips – if love this ain't,

then life deserves an Oscar for that act.
And Tom, ignorant, blissful, he kiss back.

Tom Thomson in Triumph

He survived the crash test. He survived twelve years
of intensive schooling, i.e. indoctrination
into the whys and wherefores of his nation.
He survived the phalanx of his lesser fears –
fear of flying, fear of public-speaking, fear of bears –

he survived the dart board to which he'd been tied,
blindfolded, arms outstretched – yes, *crucified* –
though he resents what goes with that vocabulary.
And he's not had the stigmata, just
astigmatism. Ah, but how he's tried –

how he's borne the stigma of intelligence,
his allergy to bullshit – his sixth sense –
waltzed to stagnant tunes 'til feet could take no more,
swayed between stalagmites on the dance hall floor.

III

Tom Thomson in Transition

Oh, he's been *here* before—this scrubbed-bright room,
this uptight crowd, in frocks of white and blue,
this frenzy of machinery . . . And he feels
a twinge of disappointment: *no more days,*
he thinks, and, granted that most days were bad
and some were simply *awful,* still, he'll miss
that daily scramble into consciousness—
or rather, he *won't* miss it, he won't feel
a single thing of any sort for any
single thing of any sort . . . Leans back.
So kind of all these folks to help me die. . .
But hey, what's with those forceps? You don't mean—
(nine breathless months have left him dulled) – A tug.
A slap. A wail. *Oh Christ no, not again . . .*

Tom Thomson in Contempt of Court

Condemned to death for crimes unspecified
(old tale – stifle a yawn) he roams his cell.
This trial of the century did not go well –
though truth be told his memory's, frankly, fried

(did the glove fit? did he attempt the Fifth?) . . .
Suspects he, though, as he stares down the years,
his court-appointed liar (who disappeared
mid-sentence) used his Harvard Law-honed gifts

to swap *his* guilt for Tom's dear innocence.
He'd like to read the transcripts, maybe watch
the T.V. movie. (Sitting on the fence –

was that his oh so Unoriginal Sin?)
"You call this *justice?*" – to which Judge say, "Hush.
We do not use the J-word round here, son."

Tom Thomson in Flanders Fields

The poppies grow, between the crosses row
by regimented row, and as they bob
pathetic Tom bobs too (no, I mean *sym-*
pathetic, for our man is overcome

and only refuge he can find is in
corrective fantasy: nineteen-sixteen,
with Thomson gun in one hand, Thomson girl
in other, he doff his cap, take his leave,

and head to France to shoot up several Germans.
(Ignore the fact that he's a pacifist,
and closest he has come to shooting gun
is his excessive use of bullet points;

this is *his* fantasy, for Christ's sake!)) Tom,
he linger for a while, then go home.

Tom Thomson in Dreamland

Flashing a smile at the security guard
She fumbles in her handbag for her gun.
Tom lights a smoke, wishing the job were done,
and sighs as rent-a-cop approaches car.
She shoots him twice before he gets too far,
then checks the grounds, to see if anyone
has heard the shots. This isn't as much fun
as he'd been promised, but it isn't hard,
and honest work's for chumps. *What did you say?*
Unusual career choice for the son
of high school teachers? It might seem that way.
I think it could happen to anyone.
He asks if she agrees. She leans to touch
his lips, gently. "Just drive. You think too much."

Tom Thomson in Disgrace

Preserved and pickled, scorned and vilified,
he hang — no, float — in his display case, as
townspeople, present, past, and future, file
through dim museum, voicing their disgust,
some pausing in mid-step to gasp and gape
(they've paid five bucks a head for just this chance)—

He'd think it quite humiliating, but
it's *hard* to think without a brain, and his
has been removed, and vatted separately.
(He sees it, bobbing, bubbling, 'cross the room.)

So empty-headed Tom lay back and sing
with all the gospel gusto he got left
the one lyric he's less than half forgot:
"If I only had a . . . " *But what come next?*

Tom Thomson in Transit

"That train's not run here for a thousand years."
(*He means a hundred, maybe?*) "They still sell
the tickets at the station, though, if any-
one would like a useless souvenir . . . "

And Tom is tempted: he do love useless things.
Remind him, they, of someone he knows well.
His wallet's stuffed with currency from all
manner of countries not in business now;

his camera aches for discontinued film.
(Ditto his typewriter & its odd ribbon).
And all his maps are maps of continents
that sank without a trace some time ago,

flora and fauna gone extinct, extinct
as Tom himself feel he must surely go.

Tom Thomson in Pain

He tastes what's coming. Feels it in his teeth:
a sharp, repugnant, piercing deep-down stab
of pain, combined with long slow feverish ache:
He is not well. Not been well for some time.
He sees a face, sometime, pass by on bus
or in a crowd at some protest event
and tiny moment of pure mind-to-mind
contact ensues: *Ah mon semblable, mon frere,
I see you feel it too.* Then looks away,
so instantaneous conspiracy of two
evades omnipresent security cam.
He tastes what's coming. Everybody knows –
though most don't know yet that they know – some change
is hurtling at them like an asteroid.

Tom Thomson in Peril

Love pushed him *hard.* Love's lawyer called him up:
relations would henceforth be broken off.
He took it bad. Was one thing when he thought
that he was through with love, but this new fact –
that *love* was through with *him* – he couldn't abide.
He whimpered, fell into retreat, recalled
his forces from the front, posted white flag
at entrance to his cabin, and retired
into a heavy sulk. Heavier still
was made that sulk by drink, which he consumed
in quantities such as t'impress a king,
perhaps even a Falstaff. When he pass by,
those who once knew him don't him recognize,
or want not to. His rough state pain their eyes.

Tom Thomson in Crisis

Did Sister rock him like a boat? Did Mother
love him deep enough? Is there a source
for all of this confusion, this remorse?
Was there some primal scene, some stab at Father –

that hateful, artful codger, that old dodge –
no, wait: he *loved* his father. Yeah, that's right;
how'd he forget? Well he's been up all night;
things slip his mind – things threaten to dislodge –

like faces, names, and places he has been,
things he's been promised, things he's promised others,
meanings of words, *tercel* and *teratoid,*

which foods he loves, and which loves to avoid,
who's living still, who's dead, and who is neither,
what the grenade say when you pull the pin.

Tom Thomson Inhospitable

Love pays a visit. Just to check on him.
Drops by quite unannounced, unfolds a chair,
sits in the corner.   Folded hands.   Expectant.
He pours a cup of tea for love.   Says nothing.
An awkward silence. What is he to say?
Remembers he what *she'd* said. "Dear, *of course*
you are enough for me—it's just—you know—
I'm never quite contented with *enough.*"
But that was then. Yes, that was long ago,
before he oversteeped the tea, before
he learned to read the fine print. Now, he know.
He tries to look like he is doing fine.
But love, contrary to the common talk,
's not blind. Love, she's got X-ray specs for eyes.

Tom Thomson in Writing

Dear S: after much thought, I think it's time
you were demoted back from hurricane
to tropical storm status. Don't take it hard.
It's not that I've recovered from your gales,

your sheets of rain like knives – my waterfront,
they say, will never really be the same
(and please don't even ask about my parks) –
but still, the worst has passed. I've opened up

a snack bar / souvenir shop at the edge
of that vast canyon you ripped in my soul.
"When life hands you a lemon, make a peach."
I'm doing fine. I'm almost in control,

some days, for several minutes at a stretch . . .
Think no more of me. Signed,

your loving wretch,

Tom Thomson in Retrospect

He had a good run. Ran like hell, in fact,
toward the wisdom and away from pain.
(Except he got them mixed up, it turned out.)
Now, worn, half-empty, wound down, he looks back

and wonders what it meant. What pattern here?
Squint, look away, look back quick: it don't change.
As bad as trying to read some night-scribed note
in rational morning sunlight, to adhere

lyrics to Schoenberg. Since when does guest of honor speak
at his own funeral? Really, what's to say?
How sum it up? He'd rather sum it *down*:
some cheap joke to send survivors on their way,

then settle back in his birch bark canoe
and let the current do what current do.

Tom Thomson in Limbo (4)

That soft sandpaper sound of the sea   is merely a cover
for what the waves are taking away.   Over and over
they wash up and lick out of being the land
on which sad Tom stand.

His task is to pretend not to see   that the world is going
somewhere beyond him and far away   that the ocean is doing
all it can to erase his dominion, and leave
nothing but ocean to breathe.

So he close his eyes and he fix his mind   on what She is
     saying
about the children they once were   who spent their nights
     playing
under a riotous sky,
as violent as wars,

                    when the sea
                    was as far away as the stars

Epilogue

Epilogue: Tom Thomson in Absentia

All things that are worth doing have been done.
(*Gravity's Rainbow*, Rothko's Chapel, Rome,
"The Second Coming," and the works of Bach . . .)
And so attempts to fill the days with hours,
the glass with wine, the empty head with noise . . .

Or: try to think up some new unknown trick,
some unanticipated twist, to add
to his old dogma, his dull doggerel . . .

Tom Thomson, in absentia, stands his ground
at end of land. Rule number ninety-three
of Robert's Rules of Ardor recommends:
lay down yourself before the dynamo.
Lay down in sand. Let ocean do its work.

Tom Thomson, undecided, ponder *that*.

Acknowledgments

Poems in this collection have appeared in the following journals:

The Antigonish Review, *The Cider Press Review*, *The Distillery*, *Exile*, *The Fiddlehead*, *Konundrum Engine*, *The Malahat Review*, *Margie: The American Journal of Poetry*, *The Nashwaak Review*, *The New Quarterly*, *Ploughshares*, *Press*, *PRISM International*, and *RATTLE*.

Thanks to the editors for allowing the republication of these poems.

★

The italicized line in "Tom Thomson Indisposed" is from the *Lament of Baba Tahir*, translated by Edward Heron-Allen and Elizabeth Curtis-Brenton.

★

For editorial advice, words of encouragement, inspiration, and various forms of support, the author would like to thank James Richardson, Paul Muldoon, Donal Power, Robert Nazarene, and Sharon Barrios.